ST. MARIA GORETTI

Saint Maria Goretti
October 16, 1890 – July 6, 1902

ST. MARIA GORETTI

IN GARMENTS ALL RED

By

Fr. Godfrey Poage, C.P.

"Who is this that cometh . . . this beauti-
ful one . . . Why then is thy apparel red,
and thy garments like theirs that tread in the
winepress?"

—Isaias 63:1-2

TAN BOOKS AND PUBLISHERS

NIHIL OBSTAT: Kilian Dooley, C.P., Ph.D.
                  Censor Deputatus

IMPRIMI POTEST: James Patrick White, C.P.
                  Provincial of Holy Cross Province
                  July 2, 1950

IMPRIMATUR: ✣ Samuel Cardinal Stritch, D.D.
                  Archbishop of Chicago
                  July 6, 1950

ISBN: 978-0-89555-615-8

Library of Congress Catalog Card No.: 97-62521

Cover illustration: The official portrait of St. Maria Goretti. Painted in 1938, it was approved as a close likeness by her mother and the postulator of her cause.

Printed and bound in the United States of America.

TAN BOOKS AND PUBLISHERS
1998

Dedicated to
Mary,
Queen of Martyrs

AUTHOR'S NOTE

My sincere gratitude goes to my confreres, especially Frs. Pierre and Dominic, whose research, many suggestions and constructive criticism played an extremely important part in this book.

CONTENTS

BEATIFICATION ADDRESS

The life story of Maria Goretti resembles very closely that of St. Agnes. The features of the Roman martyr and those of this little girl of Corinaldo shine with the same charm. The souls of both emit the same fragrance. Yet there is danger that a too superficial, too natural conception of their youthful beauty and candor will overshadow their characteristic virtue, which is *strength of soul*. Their youth sets off in a more living, more radiant light, the courage of the martyr and the courage of the virgin. Courage was both the result and safeguard of their virginity.

Those individuals err greatly who consider virginity as the effect of ignorance or the simplicity of small souls. They who smile with pity on virgins, thinking of them as passionless, ardorless or inexperienced, misjudge their true worth. How can he or she who has ceded without struggle imagine the courage required to dominate through long years, without an instant of weakness, the secret excitations and troubles of sense and heart. Since Original Sin, human nature is in a ferment, troubled by a thousand curiosities to see, to hear, to taste and to feel. Great courage is required to resist

those curiosities which present to the lips the
intoxicating cup and exude the deadly scent of the
flowers of evil. Great courage is required to live
firmly, superior to every temptation, superior to
every threat, superior to all seductive and taunting
influences amidst the baseness of the world.

Agnes in the whirl of pagan society and Maria
Goretti in the proximity of passionate, shameless
men, were neither ignorant nor insensible. They
had strong hearts, strong in that supernatural
strength whose germ every Christian received in
holy Baptism. Thanks to a diligent and sustained
education, in affectionate collaboration of parents
and children, that germ grew into manifold fruit
of virtue and blessing.

In the humble family circle where Maria Goretti
grew up, her education was simple but careful, and
she corresponded to it perfectly. The testimony of
her mother that this little girl never caused her
the least voluntary displeasure is proof enough. And
who can read without emotion the declaration of
her murderer that he never ascertained in Maria
Goretti a failing in the law of God!

Our Saint was a valiant girl. She knew, she
understood, and that is why she preferred to die.
Her twelfth year was not completed when she fell
martyred. Yet, what discernment, what prudence,
what energy she displayed! Though but a girl, conscious of danger, she watched night and day in
defense of her honor, and in persevering prayer recommended the lily of her purity to the Virgin of
virgins. No, hers was not a small, weak soul! She

is a heroine who in the clutch of a murderer and under the knife of an assassin thought not of her suffering, but resolutely repelled sin with horror.

Thank God there are still many more like her. They are more numerous than is thought or mentioned because they make no display of their seriousness and virtue, as other girls do of their levity and disorders. Raised by Christian parents, they modestly pass happy and joyful down the streets of our cities and in the byways of our countrysides. They pursue domestic, professional, scholarly and charitable duties. They know how to make their pleasing manner loved and their unbending dignity respected.

Beyond all doubt there are still very many of these girls. They would be still more numerous if there were more devoted interest and true kindness in parents, and more confident docility in children.

How many concessions are made, how many capitulations are undergone! Passing whims they are, and heedlessness quickly obliterates them at first. But their humiliating remembrance reappears later with torturing remorse, like gas bubbles coming to the surface of a stagnant pond. Their bitterness, even after pardon, is never completely assuaged. Worse still are those misfortunes that cast so many girls into the bottom of the abyss, tragedies that terminate in hopeless death, progressive falls that end in a final fall, humanly irreparable.

In view of such lamentable weaknesses, so many miserable falls, we must admire the strength of pure hearts. It is a mysterious power. It is a strength that

outstrips the limits of human nature, and often
enough the limits of ordinary Christian virtue. It is
the bond of love for the Divine Spouse. It is the
strength of the soul which spurns whoever dares test
its fidelity or threatens the purity of its affections.

Maria Goretti showed herself to be such a one
no less in her life than in her martyrdom. Shall
we then class her with Agnes and Cecilia, Cather-
ine of Siena and Therese of the Child Jesus, and
many others who, with heroic abnegation and the
blessings of their virginity, wore the nuptial ring
that bound them to their heavenly Spouse? But
Maria Goretti was only a child and there is no reason for asserting that she would have consecrated
herself to the Lord by the vow of virginity. There
is nothing to indicate that as she advanced in years
she would not have followed the path of so many
other young women who bring the flower of their
integrity to the altar in order to give God new ador-
ers through holy Matrimony—chosen members to
the human family, devoted children to the Church,
future Saints to Heaven. Yet Christ knew well that
He had chosen her for His Own. Without thought
of the future, she had given herself entirely to Him
in her heart. She desired but one thing: fidelity to
Christ at any price, even at the cost of her life.
Never for anything in the world would she violate
the Divine Law.

She was not merely an ingenuous, candid girl,
instinctively frightened at the menace of sin as at
the sight of a snake. (*Ecclus.* 21:2). She may not
be compared to the legendary ermine that permit-

ted itself to be killed rather than soil its paw on the muddy road. She was not guided simply by natural sentiment of reserve. Though still very young, we can catch a glimpse in her of a deep, intense love for Our Divine Redeemer. She had not yet learned to read. Poverty and a distance kept her from school. But her love knew neither difficulty nor distance. She set about her household tasks more courageously and hurried off to attend Catechism lessons far away. In order to receive her Eucharistic Jesus, she did not hesitate to travel a long dusty road in midsummer under a scorching sun. "I don't know at what time tomorrow I will receive Holy Communion," she said one day. That tomorrow was to come, and that Holy Communion. But what a tomorrow! and what a Communion! The very afternoon of that day on which she spoke those words, she shed her blood in order to remain faithful to the Spouse of virgins.

It is not yet a half-century since the pathetic death of Maria Goretti. The period has been one seething with stormy vicissitudes and sudden revolts. Radical transformations have upset the life of our young girls and women. We have fully pointed out on other occasions how within the past fifty years, woman has departed from the retirement and reserve that formerly characterized her life and has launched out into the domain of public life, including military service. That transformation has taken place with pitiless speed.

Lest such deep and speedy alternation effect most grave consequences to the religion and morals

of woman, it is necessary at the same time and in
equal degree to strengthen in her those deep per-
sonal and supernatural values that shone in our
Saint. There must be a spirit of faith and modesty—not mere natural modesty and decency—but
a carefully cultivated Christian virtue. Those who
have at heart the welfare of human society, as well
as the temporal and eternal salvation of woman,
must resolutely demand that public morality pro-
tect the honor and dignity of woman. What is the
present situation? Are we wrong in affirming that
in this regard perhaps no epoch has failed as ours
in its duty toward woman?

Thus the cry of our Saviour rises to our lips:
"Woe to the world because of scandals." (*Matt.*
18:7). Woe to those guilty perverters—authors of
corrupt novels, newspapers, periodicals, theatres,
films, indecent styles! Woe to those young men
who, with artful and thoughtless cruelty, introduce
deadly infection into a virgin heart! Woe to those
fathers and mothers lacking in energy and prudence, who cede to the caprices of their children
and surrender that paternal authority written on
the brow of man and wife as a reflection of the
Divine Majesty.

Woe also to that multitude of Christians in name
only, who could take a stand and would see legions
of upright and virtuous followers mass behind them
ready to battle scandal by every means! Legal justice punishes the slayer of a child, and it has a
duty to do so. But what human legislation could
or would dare, if it chose to do so, punish those

who furnished the weapon to the slayer's hand, those who encouraged him therein, or were indifferent, or even, with indulgent smile, let him be? And yet they are really the more guilty. The terrible justice of God weighs heavily on them, those willful perverters or indolent accomplices!

Has human power, then, no strength to move and convert those corrupt and corrupting hearts? Has it no strength to open the eyes and arouse those many careless, timid Christians from their torpor? We hope this martyr's blood and the tears of her repentant and penitent murderer will perform that miracle!

Our hope is not in vain. Thus, we do not hesitate to repeat here the words of the Apostle Paul: "Where sin abounded, grace did more abound." (*Rom.* 5:20). Behold the Church! Now the ranks of those who believe, who pray, who impose heavy sacrifices on themselves grow and form even among the youth! They squarely reject what God wills not to be. They are restless until they have brought back to Christ and His law their friends and associates who have become estranged from God. They are Our comfort and Our joy.

Full of such confidence, let us raise up our eyes to Heaven and consider the resplendent host of those who have washed their robes in the Blood of the Lamb, that host led by the Virgin of virgins. Let us call upon their intercession. Let us unite our humble prayers to theirs in order to bring down upon the earth the abundant shower of grace that cleanses and strengthens.

As a pledge of that grace We accord you with all Our heart Our Apostolic Blessing.

—Pope Pius XII
April 27, 1947
Beatification of Maria Goretti

PROLOGUE

They say that if you go from Rome to Nettuno by way of Campo Morto and Ferriere, you will hear everybody along the way speaking of Maria Goretti. Through that countryside she has become legendary. The old people remember her; the young have learned to love her.

One old lady tells us proudly that she made her First Communion with Maria. Another met the Saint many times on market day. A farmer claims she came to him, a few days before her death, to return a sickle that Alessandro Serenelli had borrowed. A seamstress remembers Maria coming to her mother's shop to try on a dress the very morning of the day Alessandro attacked her. Not yet a half century after her death, Maria Goretti lives in the hearts of her people.

When I asked her neighbor, Theresa Cimarelli, about her, she exclaimed: "Madonna mia! I used to see her every day as she passed by the door to get water from the well. But she never stopped. She was a serious girl. She came and went quickly and busily, and there was no reproach when we nicknamed her *the little old lady*.

"Maria was always modest and reserved. We all

liked her, and deep down we admired her. She was more religious than the rest of us. I was just a girl then, and would that I had followed her example! But at that age most of us are senseless. We scarcely know what we are doing. We seek pleasure and popularity. We permit ourselves to be distracted from better things."

She hesitated a moment and sighed. She seemed to have more to say, but refrained.

"Come in," she invited, "and meet Domenico." I needed no urging, for Theresa Cimarelli and her brother had lived through the events of our story and were witnesses of many of its details.

I sat down at the simple wooden table and looked about the plainly furnished room. Theresa went to the back door and called: "Domenico . . . Domenico!"

There was no reply, but the wood chopping in a nearby shed ceased. The old lady then drew out a jug of wine and set glasses on the table. In a moment Domenico entered.

Domenico was up in years and walked with a stoop. The sun had tanned his skin. His blue work-clothes gave off the pungent odor of sheep. He offered me his hand in honest welcome, drew up a chair and filled the glasses with the cool, sparkling wine. Theresa then explained to him my interest in the life of Maria Goretti and urged him to help her retell the story.

The pleasure of these two friends of Maria having a foreigner in their home and being able to retell the drama they had witnessed was all too evident. They seemed to relive those tragic scenes. No detail was omitted.

Theresa and Domenico have not left Ferriere since Maria's death, and I can only guess the hundreds of times they have gone over the terrible story together in the past forty-five years. All I did was listen. They told the tale from beginning to end and concluded with these words:

"The day of the burial of Maria—and it was a real triumph—the whole populace of Nettuno accompanied the body to the cemetery. Her mother, Assunta, came back to Ferriere. She did not stay long. You understand. She could no longer live in the house that recalled such sad memories. So she left this region and returned to Corinaldo with her children. Old Serenelli disappeared, too. No one ever heard of him again. The Ferriere farm was once more abandoned and once more known as 'the old cheese factory.'"

"What about Alessandro?" I asked. I was eager to know how he had paid for his crime.

"Alessandro!" said Domenico. "That is a whole story in itself! First of all, he was imprisoned at Nettuno. They then transferred him to the Regina Coeli at Rome, where his trial began. I was called in as witness. Alessandro was arrogant and cynical before his judges. He denied up and down that he had anything to do with the crime. He pretended that he was the object of grave injustice and was highly indignant that anyone should accuse him of such a transgression. But the evidence was overwhelming. Though he put on a brave front, he was not able to escape, and finally made an avowal of guilt. Then, to influence the judges, he tried to hide behind the curtain of insanity, calling in the cases of his mother and brother. Doctors examined him and declared he was responsible for his own actions. But since he was a minor, he was sentenced to only thirty years of hard labor.

"I heard that he was sent first to the penitentiary of Noto in Sicily. It was said that in the beginning of his term he seemed happy as a bird in its cage. He even composed a song with the refrain:

'Take courage, Serenelli,
Banish your fears,
You'll be welcomed home with cheers.'

"His conscience did not seem to be troubled with remorse, until one day a priest came to see him. As the guards brought Alessandro in for the talk, fierce anger seized hold of him and he yelled wildly: 'It was all your fault that I lost her! You and your teachings!'

"The priest tried to reason with him, appealing to God's infinite mercy and Maria's own generous pardon. But Alessandro only howled like a maniac and lunged at the priest. As the guards pulled him away, the priest said, 'Soon, Alessandro, you will want me. Maria will see to that.'

" 'Never,' the prisoner screamed. 'I'll never want you, never!'

"In the days that followed Alessandro could not sleep. He grew nervous and lost his appetite. Then one night, in the solitude of Alessandro's cell,

Maria appeared to him. Terrified, he screamed for the guards. When they arrived, he was almost incoherent.

" 'I saw her! I saw her!' he gasped in great excitement. 'I saw Maria dressed in dazzling white, gathering beautiful lilies in a garden and handing them to me. As I took them from her outstretched hands, they were transformed into small lights that glowed like candles. Call the priest! Bring me the priest!'

"It was now the jailers' turn to laugh. 'Write to the priest if you have something to say,' they answered callously. So Alessandro knelt on the floor of his cell and scrawled the following note:

> 'I am deeply sorry for what has happened. I have taken the life of an innocent girl whose one aim was to save her purity, shedding her blood rather than give in to my sinful desires. I publicly retract the evil I have done and beg pardon of God and of the stricken family. One hope encourages me—that I also may one day obtain God's pardon, as so many others have.
>
> Alessandro Serenelli
> November 10, 1910'

"This note from Alessandro only confirmed our belief that Maria was a Saint, a real martyr. The word of how she had died passed throughout the country, and people started making pilgrimages to her tomb. We prayed to her and asked for cures . . . and miracles were performed."

I looked skeptical. Domenico noted my astonishment and continued.

"I saw a boy of Nettuno brought to the cemetery by his mother. He was eaten away by consumption, a wasted child, Hermano by name. They prayed at Maria's grave, and the boy left the cemetery cured. From that day forward he grew strong and healthy, and when he was twenty, he was drafted for military service.

"I heard also of a man in Rome who was instantly cured of an internal abscess by calling on Maria. His doctor attested to the fact. I could tell you of many other incidents equally as marvelous; for instance, the Lady Miscetti, who was to undergo an operation, was cured of a cyst in her thyroid gland after praying to Maria. Then, too, a Sicilian priest was freed of a serious kidney condition by the same prayer. But what does it matter after all? Miracles don't change anything. When one has chosen to die rather than to offend God, one is a martyr and that's that! That's why our little Maria is a Saint today."

I was going from one surprise to another. The good Domenico seemed to know his history. He was full of his theme. He was not just talking. He was expatiating with remarkable ease. I began to perceive that he had been more closely involved in the affair, though I did not know where he was leading: "Did you say she has been canonized?" I asked innocently.

He was more astonished than I. "You mean you think she doesn't deserve it?" he asked.

"No," I replied, "but why has it taken so long?"

"Rome," he answered, "moves slowly in canonizing Saints. There are inquiries, depositions, discussions . . . and then all the data is put away in the archives. Then some fine day, the case is taken up again. New inquests, new depositions, new discussions are brought forth. This time it seems we have something. It is going to succeed. And then . . . disappointment! The devil's advocate finds an objection: Maria should have disclosed her secret . . . she hesitated before pardoning her assassin . . . she may have provoked him. Such false reasons hold up the process. Thus we have to be patient for years. But the Church knows best.

"I was called in several times," Domenico continued, "to testify. Police, doctors, nurses were also called in—everyone, in fact, who had something to say. Assunta, naturally, was the first defendant of her daughter. We were all of one mind. Maria was innocent; she had given proof of her heroic courage. But that was not enough. One witness was wanting—the only one able to settle the question, her murderer, Alessandro!

"After thirty-five years, he came back to Corinaldo, a changed man. Maria's prayers had won him completely. His prison sentence had been served, and he wanted to repair the evil of his crime. He who formerly had taken every means to exonerate himself now humbly admitted his guilt. It is no small thing when a criminal rises to the defense of his victim. He affirmed that she had been altogether innocent. She had opposed his brutal passion with all her strength. Finally, he obtained what he sought—her vindication.

"He even went further than that, and on Christmas Eve of 1937 begged pardon of Assunta. The old mother's voice broke as she fought back the tears: 'Maria forgave you, Alessandro,' she answered, 'so how could I possibly refuse?'

"The following morning, Christmas Day, the parish Church at Corinaldo was filled to overflowing as Assunta and Alessandro entered side by side. A hush fell on everyone. At the Communion rail, Alessandro turned and all eyes were upon him.

"'I have sinned deeply,' he said. 'I have murdered an innocent girl who loved virtue more than life. May God forgive me! I beg your pardon!'

"After this, I heard that Alessandro had retired to a Capuchin Monastery of Ascoli, where he put on the habit of a tertiary. He's working there now as gardener, tending the flowers. Lilies are his favorites . . ."

Domenico seemed to have finished his tale. I had listened with intense interest. What a story! And yet, all so true.

I knew from a friend of mine who had been present what popular enthusiasm accompanied the Canonization on June 24, 1950. In front of that great throng, an old lady, Assunta, had the place of honor. She raised her head with tear-filled eyes and saw the veil removed from the picture of Maria just as His Holiness Pope Pius XII proclaimed her to be a Saint.

The excited Holy Year throng behind expressed her thoughts. "There she is . . . Maria Goretti . . . St. Maria Goretti!" Thus the drama of Ferriere has terminated in the glory of the Vatican!

"For me," mused Domenico, "she will always be our little Maria. I wouldn't know how to call her otherwise. You understand, we were her neighbors. We lived in the house next to hers. I was twenty years old when she died."

Domenico fell to silent musing. He was tired reminiscing. The village clock struck eleven. I was about to leave when the door opened. A little girl looked in. At the sight of me, she hesitated, doubtful as to whether she should enter or withdraw. A great straw hat haloed her head. She wore a blue and white summer dress, which scarcely reached her knees. Her bare arms were tanned with the sun.

"Angelina, come in and speak to Father," said Domenico. "Don't stand there gaping."

"This is my granddaughter," he explained. The little girl seemed timid, frightened at my presence. But she came over and shook hands with smiling grace. Then she went out by the back door.

I rose and thanked Domenico and Theresa for their kindness and hospitality. But for them, my story would have been incomplete. I paused a moment on the threshold to adjust my eyes to the burning sunlight, and then set off resolutely for the long, hot walk to Nettuno. Maria had made the journey before me, and it seemed I was following her. No one else was on the road at that time of day, and I walked alone with my thoughts.

Maria . . . Angelina . . . girl of yesterday . . . youngster of today.

Styles have changed. The light dress and straw hat have replaced the heavy skirts and shawls. Long braided hair has given place to a simple cut and combing. Adornments and mannerisms have altered. But deep down there has been no transformation. A girl's real beauty is still within. It is a thing of her soul, shining through her pure eyes and radiating her whole body. It is something by which she makes men aware of the truth and beauty and goodness of God by reflecting that beauty and goodness in herself.

At Nettuno, in the Basilica of Our Lady of Grace, I visited the shrine where the body of Maria Goretti is preserved. A young man was there, kneeling in prayer. He thought he was alone, and I saw him lean over reverently to kiss the marble in front of her reliquary. Then he blessed himself and left, buoyed up with the confidence that Maria, the new patroness of Catholic youth, would help him gain a victory over himself.

This is more than enough for the triumphs of today! Let us go back some fifty years to the more important story of how Maria actually won her victory over sin . . .

ST. MARIA GORETTI

MAP OF ITALY

SENIGALLIA
CORINALDO
ANCONA

ADRIATIC
SEA

APENNINE MOUNTAINS

ROME

CAMPO MORTO
FERRIERE
DI CONCA

ANZIO
NETTUNO

TYRRHENIAN
SEA

MEDITERRANEAN

—1—

JOURNEY FOR MARIA

"Assunta, I tell you, we'd do better to leave this place," Luigi exclaimed.

But the mother only bent over the fire and banked the embers. The flame glowed warmly. Their three children, gathered about the hearth, spread their hands to the heat. Assunta straightened up and heaved a sigh, but said nothing.

"You know, I was talking to the Cimarellis last night. They are leaving in the Spring," he continued.

It was like a shock to her! Assunta guessed immediately that her husband had reached a decision with their neighbor. He was trying to break the news gently.

For several winters now the idea of immigrating had tempted him. Luigi was a hard-working farmer, a man of action. On bad days, when snow and rain confined him to pacing the kitchen from window to door, from door to cupboard and back again, he could not help complaining about the land and climate. It was useless to argue with him, thought Assunta. She had tried it often. Early she had learned that discussion was futile. So now she was ready to accept what she could not prevent. She fought back the tears.

"Then you wish that we leave with them?" she asked.

Her voice was calm and slow. Luigi looked at her, but her eyes remained fixed on the flames. She seemed resigned. He had not expected so easy a victory.

"Yes, Assunta, we must. We can no longer remain here. Over there you will be much happier, believe me. In the neighborhood of Rome there are vacant farms and lands to be leased. We will find ourselves something worthwhile."

The storm door slammed! A blizzard was at its height. Snow was falling heavily. Winters are severe in the neighborhood of Ancona, and though one might well love that country for its pure air and steep pathways, when storms arise and fuel is low, it can become a land of misery.

There was a long silence in the Goretti home. The two boys and Maria continued to warm themselves by the fire. Assunta passed a damp cloth over the table she had just cleared.

She was a farm-bred, healthy woman, in her early thirties, slender still, in spite of the loose skirts that hung in folds about her. Luigi watched her work. Her slow movements spoke more eloquently than words of the painful fatigue and discouragement. He understood that she had just accepted the hardest sacrifice of her life. She was attached to this village, where she had always lived, where her parents lay buried. She had known no other horizon than these mountain slopes. With him it was different. As a soldier, he had traveled over the Apennines and through the fertile plains beyond.

"Why should one kill oneself in these mountains steeped in rock, rubble and harsh weather for reasons of sentiment?" he had asked himself time and time again.

The cold weather whistled under the door. The three youngsters were becoming sleepy by the hearth. Assunta was now washing the dishes. Luigi's anguish mounted. With his fingernail he scraped a hole in the frost on the windowpane. A huge blanket of white covered everything, and the snow continued. There was no end of it. It was up to the height of the well now. The stone bench and the rose bushes were buried from sight.

Then a little hand slipped into his own. He lowered his eyes, and the hard lines in his face softened. It was his darling Maria, who had come to press herself to his side. He kissed her forehead and ran his fingers through her long chestnut hair. This little girl of six was his favorite. She had indeed a temper that broke out occasionally, but in her calmer moments she was so affectionate and sweet! She turned her limpid eyes to her father and begged him to take her in his arms. Her rosy cheeks reminded Luigi of warmth and sunshine out beyond the Apennines on the shores of the Mediterranean.

At length the winter passed. The snow melted and rivers rushed madly to the sea. Then one bright morning, Luigi loaded his cart, hitched up his oxen and drove slowly away from Corinaldo. All he had left was his household goods and a few hundred lire, for he had sold his cottage and his field. The two boys, Angelo and Marino, age nine and four, played amid the bundles of belongings. Assunta, sitting in front with Maria and Luigi, was nursing a newborn child, Alessandro.

The Cimarelli cart followed behind them. Domenico and Luigi had always been close neighbors. Theresa and Assunta, friends from childhood, would not have wished to be separated for anything in the world.

Together they crossed the Apennines. Together they followed the winding road toward Rome. It took them several weeks to make the two-hundred mile journey by ox cart. At times Luigi walked behind, deep in thought.

Maria watched the white mountain peaks fade in the distance. In her young mind was impressed forever that last picture—the great snowy heights of Corinaldo reaching heavenward.

—2—

HOME IN THE SWAMPLAND

They arrived at last. But Luigi soon began to think it were better had they never come!

For two days the Gorettis and Cimarellis wandered the streets of Rome. To these simple farmers, the great city was a universe. They knew not where to go, helplessly wandering about, retracing their steps. A dozen times they repassed the same place without noticing it. They visited churches, prayed before the Virgin's statues, lit candles, called on the Saints. Yet, despite the prayers, a pitiless fate seemed to steer them toward their ruin.

From a chance acquaintance they learned that Count Mazzoleni owned rich lands in the neighborhood of Nettuno. He rented them out, they were told, at a reasonable price. Or better still, he ceded them on a profit-sharing basis. They were supposed to be good farms, lands that furnished a rich livelihood regardless of the year. There were swamps there, too, and the climate was damp. But that should not stop anyone.

"Why not go there?" the stranger suggested. "You can see for yourself. I know the place. It belongs to the district of Conca. Stop off at Ferriere and inquire. They'll tell you where it is."

Luigi and Domenico thanked the good man and set off without further delay. If only they had known what lay in store for them.

As they approached the marshes, the air became heavy. Heavy, too, was the cart in which the children, tired of their cramped quarters, began to complain. Maria alone was patient and quiet. With her little legs hanging over the back of the cart, she thought on many things. The heavy wheels rumbled on the pavement. She was not worried or concerned about where this strange adventure would end, and it little mattered to her where they would be by dusk. She noted that they were leaving the city. Little by little, all that great world was left behind—its many people, its beautiful churches, its great houses stuck close one upon the other. Soon they were out in the open country, and vineyards and fields of wheat and corn appeared. It was hot and she was thirsty, but father had said there would be no stopping. The oxen trudged along. Luigi was whistling in contentment. Domenico cracked his whip.

When they saw afar off the first houses of Ferriere, they sighed with relief. The journey had been long. Luigi stood up and peered through the trees at a turn in the road. He noticed that there was no church spire. But then, you cannot expect everything. He urged on his beast, and in short time they were in the midst of the poor village. No shops welcomed them. Not a door nor window was ajar along the dirty road. It was siesta time and apparently strictly observed. Luigi knocked three times at one of the houses. There was no reply, but movements within gave hope of an answer. The door was unbolted, and a wrinkled old lady peered through the opening with blinded eyes.

"Could you tell me where to find Count Mazzoleni's farm?" Luigi asked.

The old woman was not quite awake, and it was necessary to repeat louder.

"Oh, you mean the old cheese factory!" She took a step forward in the doorway. "It's over there on your left. The last place, you can't miss it."

They found the place all right. It was an oblong, tile-roofed building set on a rise of ground. All about it was flat, low-lying, swampy farm. The children piled out of the cart and began exploring the yard. The heat was intense. There were no trees about the place, nor shade of any description. Everything seemed dead. The hen house was empty and the stone watering-trough scorched and dry.

Luigi and Assunta looked over the farm, visited the stable and shed, went through the kitchen and two rooms of the house, then climbed the stairway to the upper floor. They met neither dog nor cat nor any other living thing. And thus without arousing anyone they took possession of Ferriere farm.

Next day the arrangements were settled. Luigi and Domenico became share-croppers of Count Mazzoleni. The Cimarellis took over the house adjacent to that of the Gorettis. They were not partners—just neighbors.

Assunta very quickly had the place cleaned and

swept. Misery was stalking them, but hope was adamant.

It was a dangerous situation for this family, accustomed to the invigorating air of the mountain heights, to become stranded on the edge of the Pontine Marshes, which were damp and unhealthy, a hotbed of malaria.

But Luigi set about his work courageously. No longer was he working with little plots, one higher than the other, as at Corinaldo. Here, low-lying fields and meadows stretched out in flat panorama.

For the past three years the property had been neglected. The preceding hired man had lived on the spontaneous yield of the ground, without taking any pains to develop its resources. Neglected ditches failed to carry off the excess water which spread out in pools over the land. With great energy, Luigi tried to bring the land under control. Ditch digging occupied him for the rest of the summer. The water seeped off and plowing began. By Fall he was able to sow eight acres in wheat and barley. But such rugged labor in the heat and damp of the Pontine Marshes was too much, even for the robust farmer of the mountain country. His strength was undermined.

The first attacks of fever were light, and he paid no attention to them. Assunta urged him to rest. But Luigi could not remain idle and set out to work as though nothing were the matter. A few days later, coughing commenced and then he was obliged to admit his defeat. For a week he lay in bed suffering from bronchial trouble. But no sooner was he

up again than he set about working on the road-
way, and for two weeks hauled rocks and stone from
the quarry. Then hedge trimming and firewood took
up his attention. On through the winter he worked
desperately, in spite of continued weakness and a
bothersome cough. As soon as the land was in
shape, he undertook repair of the buildings. Repair
of roofs, cleaning of lofts, partitions in the stable
. . . one task followed another, one project gave
rise to others. He went and came without rest—
without thought of the dread disease that was
undermining his health.

Meanwhile, in the home, Maria was maturing
rapidly. Her eyes were opening upon life, her hands
learning the family arts. Before too long, death
would come to pay a visit, and hardship already
hovered over Ferriere.

COMING OF THE SERENELLIS

Harvest time came. Luigi sharpened his sickle and set out early. He was counting on doing it alone. If he hired no one to help bring in the crop, there would be more sustenance for his family. That was his last imprudence.

In the first days, all went well. The sheaves, accumulating behind him, lent ardor to his task. For hours at a time he bent over the furrows, dripping with sweat, not pausing an instant. It was foolish for him to work so hard. Each evening he came back more worn out than the preceding day. He went to bed with hardly any supper. At this rate he could not carry on. Toward the end of the week he became dizzy, and one whole afternoon he lay helpless in the field. When he finally struggled back to the house, he was breathing heavily.

The next morning he was unable to go to Sunday Mass at Campo Morto. Monday he was prostrate in bed, unable even to think of returning to work. That same morning, Count Mazzoleni came to examine his Ferriere farm. He was quite dismayed to see Luigi's harvest delayed more than that of his neighbors. Their crops were practically in the barn, while Luigi's crops, half-mowed, lay limp upon the field. The grain was over-ripe, and any day it might fall. The Count could not understand why the bundles had not been gathered up. Luigi was apparently lying down on the job. Mazzoleni was quite angry and resolved to let his hired man know his mind. He stormed into the house and vented his wrath upon the sick man.

Luigi knew not what to reply. He tried to explain and finished by admitting that he would not be able to bring in the harvest. He would have to have help, at least for a time. After that he would be able to maintain the farm.

"I'll send you two men tomorrow," Count Mazzoleni cut in. "The harvest can't wait any longer! Giovanni Serenelli and his son came to me this morning looking for work. I'll send them to you, and you can make your own arrangements."

Luigi remained silent. His weakness and the thought of having to share the fruits of his labors were heavy upon him. Whatever the price, there was no other solution. It remained to be seen how Assunta would take it. He called his wife and decided to tell her, but then his courage failed him. She, too, was overburdened with work. A few weeks ago she had given birth to Ersilia and was too occupied with the children even to sit down for supper. Luigi watched her straighten up the sickroom and kept silent. He realized how two more men in the house would be a terrible burden on her. She certainly would not agree to lodge and feed them.

Slowly plans turned about in his mind. He could

lend them his ox-cart to take them to Nettuno each evening and back again in the morning. Or again, he might find them lodging in the village some-where. But each idea was so impractical—lack of time, lack of lodging. Besides, he was not able to hire them at a fixed salary. He had not fifty lire to his name. Of necessity, he must take them into partnership and cede them part of the house. Then another series of insurmountable difficulties crowded in upon him.

Luigi was not well, and his troubles wore him down. When the children were asleep, Assunta returned. The husband and wife said their evening prayers together and put out the light. "Tomorrow," Luigi thought, "I'll tell her," and made a great effort to lose his troubles in sleep.

Giovanni Serenelli and his son knocked on the door early next morning and introduced themselves in the provincial speech of Ancona. Surprise and embarrassment yielded to the tale of hardship and want. At first, Assunta did not understand the object of their visit. As she dressed the children in the bedroom, she followed the conversation in the kitchen. They spoke in her native dialect and of persons and places that were dear to her. Gio-vanni seemed to be about sixty. He had an easy flow of speech and knew how to touch Luigi with the recital of his miseries. His wife had died in an insane asylum. Another son was still there. The other children were married and settled in the region about Ancona. He was left alone and pen-niless with this youngest son, Alessandro. Luigi looked at the young man. He was well-built and apparently strong beyond his eighteen years.

At length they came to the vital question. Giovanni proposed sharing work and profits on a fifty-fifty basis. "Count Mazzoleni," he said, "proposed that arrangement yesterday evening. Besides, we don't need much in the way of lodging. We can all eat together and we'll get along fine."

Old Serenelli was very amicable and would not hear of detailed conditions. What he wanted most, he said, was a home and family life; he had suffered enough loneliness since the death of his wife.

Luigi was touched with sympathy and gave in. Even Assunta did not dare interfere. The deal was concluded, and the newcomers began their work immediately.

The following Monday Luigi accompanied Giovanni and his son to Nettuno to get their furniture and belongings. The trio returned together. Two iron beds were set up in a room Assunta had prepared. Their meatloaf and bread were put in the cupboard with the Goretti food supply. Their clothing was hung in the family press. In the evening they supped together. The common life had begun.

—4—

MISUNDERSTANDING AND WARNING

For the first few days, even the first weeks, all went well in the Goretti home. It is rather easy to get along with those who come from one's own native place and speak one's own dialect. Giovanni and Alessandro were out to work early—the harvest was under control. Assunta prepared her best meals. The children were happy, and after work hours they played with the new boy. He taught them how to catch birds. He could make reed whistles. They were fascinated by the things he could do. A bit of joy returned to the Goretti household. Hope lighted again. The sheaves of wheat piled up in the barn. "Better days are coming," thought Luigi.

As long as the heavy work lasted there was no misunderstanding or discussion. The newcomers were hard workers. They lost no time, and in the evening they were too tired to wrangle. After the harvest, the sale of the produce and the plowing kept them busy.

Then winter set in, with its long days of rain and idleness. Time hung on their hands. Old Serenelli took to drinking. The habit that poverty had driven out reasserted itself. The wine of those southern lands is strong—and though he rarely became drunk, his character soured. He was irritable, overbearing and dissatisfied.

Alessandro, too, began to show evil tendencies. Having lost his mother in childhood, he had a void in his heart. He resented the fact that he had been left to the careless tutelage of a cousin—then to an aunt. His own father had taken no interest in him. At the age of twelve, he had found work with the stevedores. In that first apprenticeship, he had learned the foulest language of the sea and would curse and swear on the least provocation. At fifteen he led a lonely life. His character was warped, and the family life at Ferriere could not alter it.

He became increasingly taciturn, shunned the children, had no friends and visited no one. When the others went to Mass at Nettuno or Campo Morto, he went off by himself. Assunta noted that he went regularly to a news-stand and came back with a bundle of lurid magazines. He would then lock himself in his room and would not come out for the rest of the day. This brooding had an evil effect on him. His manner darkened, and something of the sneak appeared in his look. Assunta became alarmed. She wondered what was going on in his soul . . . and soon, to her grief, she would learn.

The next time Assunta cleaned Alessandro's room, she saw with dismay that he had clipped a number of immodest pictures from the magazines and had hung them about his bed. Her first impulse was to seize them and put them in the fire. But she refrained. That would only start a quarrel and bring more trouble into the home. Perhaps it would be better not to interfere. She was not, after all, responsible for his conduct. His father knew of these things, and it was up to him to take action. But she resolved to watch over her eldest, Angelo. He was approaching his teens, and the evil influence of a good-for-nothing might lead him astray. She strictly forbade him to enter the Serenelli room. She did not breathe a word, even to Luigi, of her discovery.

Things went from bad to worse. Luigi suspected that Giovanni was slyly disposing of grain from their common store. That needed to be settled. He proposed separation in equal lots of the produce. The terms of agreement between friends would have to be made practical. Giovanni became exacting. There was quarreling and harsh words. It might have gone to blows if Luigi had not ceded for the sake of peace in the home.

The poor man sighed for his mountain home. He regretted especially having admitted these two men to his fellowship. If he could only stand up against them and maintain his paternal authority! But he felt weak in the face of them and capitulated. Malaria had undermined his strength, and during the winter it accomplished its work.

By spring a subtle apathy laid hold of him. Chills came and went at intervals, but he held on stubbornly. He tried not to complain and went out to work with apparently the same ardor, only he never seemed to urge on his oxen as before. In the evening he sat down as soon as he entered the house, but ate very little. Assunta noted his exhaustion, his pallid complexion and the dark circles under his eyes, but what was to be done? She dared not say anything. The contract to work must be kept.

Toward the end of April he went to bed. The sickness was making great strides. Maria ran over to Nettuno for quinine, but it brought little relief. In less than ten days Luigi's strength was gone. His breathing was quick and measured. His pale arms lay limp on the covers. The little children, without too well understanding the significance, knelt about the bed in prayer. Maria especially, his own little Maria, redoubled her fervent prayers and wept in silence.

One afternoon, Luigi had a spasm of suffocation. He threw his head back and remained still, his hands tense. Assunta was alarmed. Giovanni and Alessandro were out in the fields. She sent Maria in haste to get help. The little girl hurried out and notified all the neighbors. When she got back, Luigi had regained consciousness. She went over to his bed. A smile of tenderness played about his lips, and with his icy hand he touched the moist forehead of his darling.

"How warm you are, Maria, where have you been?" The little girl hesitated a moment and then whispered:

"It is nothing, Papa, I just ran in from outside." And she took the trembling hand of her father in her own little warm hands and kissed it.

A few days later Luigi asked for the priest. This was journey's end. The neighbors assembled silently in the room of the dying man. Assunta had placed a crucifix and two candles on the white covering of a little table. Holy water and a twig were there too, with a few pieces of cotton. All knelt to recite the Rosary while waiting for the priest. Luigi followed the prayers. His lips moved and he tried to answer. Then he drifted off in sleep, and in his last dream memories returned.

He saw again the low cottages of Corinaldo with their red tile roofs on the mountain slope. He saw the lofty bell-tower from where the Adriatic was visible. Wind whistled through the valley and shook the olive trees. Sheets were spread beneath the branches to catch the precious fruit. The oil-press turned in the yard. Again he climbed the pathway to his field, but it was much steeper now and his breath came short. Pictures became jumbled in his imagination.

He opened his eyes. The candles were lit. He looked about at all the neighbors praying. He seemed to be looking for someone. All were hushed in silence. Finally his gaze set, the eyes of a dying man, glowing like embers on the hearth of a darkened room. Giovanni and Alessandro were standing there in the doorway.

Luigi wanted to cry out but was unable to. He tried to rise, but fell back on the pillow. Assunta leaned over him. He murmured in a broken voice that only she could hear. "Assunta . . . go back . . . to Corinaldo."

When the priest came, Luigi was breathing lightly, but he was still fully conscious. They were left alone. Then he received the Last Sacraments and answered to the Last Blessing. He seemed calmer now. Yet from time to time he raised himself and repeated with suppliant, haggard eyes: "Assunta . . . go back to Corinaldo . . . go back to Corinaldo."

Some thought he was delirious. That same evening he died.

—5—

MARIA'S HAPPIEST DAY

"Mother, when will I make my First Communion? I can no longer live without Jesus."

It was the month of June, 1901. Maria Goretti would soon be eleven. At that time it was not customary to receive before twelve, except in rare cases. God knows with what ardor the lovely girl longed for that happy day. Divine grace was working within her soul with such strength that it had already aroused an insatiable hunger for the Holy Eucharist.

"Your First Communion? But, my child," replied the mother sadly, "how can you do it? You can't read . . . and I have nothing to pay for your dress and slippers. We have no time to spare; there is so much work to be done here."

"At that rate, I can never make my First Communion," Maria pleaded, "and I want Jesus so badly."

"What can your poor mother do? It hurts me to see you grow up without instruction, like the animals of the field."

"Well, Mother, if that is the case, don't worry. God will see to it. There is a lady at Conca, Elvira Schiassi, who can read. I will hurry through the housework, if you will let me go to Conca to learn the Catechism. Besides, Dom Paliana comes from Citerna every Sunday to teach religion. He will instruct me with the other children preparing for First Communion."

The mother consented to the proposal, and for eleven months Maria prepared for that great moment when Jesus would come to her as the Bread of Life. Her First Communion was a triumph of her tenacious piety over the rather rigid piety of her mother. Without that tenacity and constancy she probably would have died without ever having received.

Once the decision was made, Assunta saw to it that her daughter received instruction. Sometimes she took Maria to Campo Morto or to Conca. Again, she would send Maria to the Passionist Fathers at Nettuno, that she might learn to go to Confession and prepare for Holy Communion.

From that day Maria intensified her piety and recollection, her obedience to her mother and her care of brothers and sisters. Playthings and nice clothes had no interest for her. She was busy preparing her soul for her Jesus. One day she returned home beaming. "Mama mia! Dom Signori said I would make my First Communion on the Feast of Corpus Christi."

As the great day approached, Assunta began to wonder if her daughter were really ready. Did she understand the act she was about to perform? Poor Assunta was troubled with anxieties and responsibilities for her Maria. Finally, she set the matter before Dom Temistocle Signori, the Archpriest of Nettuno.

The wise and holy Dom Signori examined the girl and, filled with admiration at her answers, expressed his complete satisfaction. "Be at ease, good mother. Your daughter is very well prepared. Put away all your vain fears and confide her to Mary Immaculate. Place her under the Virgin's protecting mantle and have no fear."

Assunta followed the priest's advice, and years later she was able to say: "My Maria made her First Communion like a Saint."

All Ferriere hamlet had part in her adornment for that great event. One furnished slippers, another the veil, a third a crown of flowers. Assunta offered her own earrings to enhance the beauty of her daughter. Maria was wrapped in expectation. With tears of joy and compunction she knelt before her mother, her brothers, her sisters and her neighbors, to ask pardon of her faults.

Twelve other girls and two boys composed the First Communion class. A Passionist, Father Jerome, from the Retreat of Our Lady of Grace at Nettuno, was the celebrant. During the sermon he addressed the children with fervent words on the great love of Jesus for them. He exhorted them warmly ever to preserve their souls pure and innocent, and *to die rather than commit a mortal sin*. He recommended to them the practice of saying three Hail Marys each evening in honor of Mary Immaculate.

These warm exhortations added fuel to the already growing flame of love in the heart of Maria.

What were her words of love to Jesus? What did the Divine Host say to her at this great tryst of two inflamed hearts? The glow of her countenance, the modesty and gravity of her bearing, showed only a feeble glimmer of the Light that burned within. While the other children hastened to the sacristy after Mass to thank Father Jerome, Maria remained behind, wrapped in a silent intimate colloquy with God.

A light cloud of sadness veiled the complete joy of this day . . . the remembrance of her dead father. Maria loved her hard-working father as only an eldest daughter of the poor can love her parent. The hardships of his life were ever present to her mind. His great sacrifice and pain at having to quit this life before having provided for his family were deeply impressed on her memory. Each evening before retiring to rest, she had said the entire Rosary for the repose of his soul. Whenever she had passed by the cemetery where he lay, she paused to say a Hail Mary for him. And now, while furtive tears stole down her cheeks, from her heart a fervent prayer went heavenward for her dear father.

Throughout the whole day Maria remained under the spell of the Princely visit of that morning. A visible joy beamed in her countenance and colored all her words and actions. Maria, ever docile and obliging, now became ardent in her endeavor to serve and to please. The good Assunta took the occasion to urge her daughter on: "You have received Jesus today. You must try ever so hard now to be good and pleasing to Him." Toward evening

Maria's thoughts started in a new direction. "Oh! When shall I be able to receive Jesus again?"

So ended the happiest day of her life. The King of Martyrs had come to nourish with His own Body and Blood this lily of purity, and the day was not far distant when He would come again and take her home with Him.

—6—

THE LITTLE WOMAN

Time passed over the grave of Luigi. Life at Ferriere became very sad. Assunta experienced many an hour of deep distress. She had hoped at first to be able to return to her native village. Deep down she had long been homesick, and besides, it was the last wish of her poor Luigi. But it was necessary to set aside this dream. How could she, with neither money nor assistance, undertake such a journey with her children? Angelo, her eldest, was scarcely thirteen. So she resigned herself to remaining at Ferriere, where Giovanni had become master. He was harsh and would not even accept her for work in the fields except on the condition that Maria, now going on twelve, take her place in the house.

Maria had become one of those children whom hardship and bitter experience of life make serious beyond their years. She went about her chores with scarcely a smile on her face, a bit of sadness in her deep brown eyes. Overnight she had changed from a laughing girl to a quiet little woman, preoccupied with her responsibilities.

Now Maria must manage the household and care for her little brothers and sisters. Meals, washing and mending occupied her from early morning to late at night. At any hour of the day she could be seen working about the kitchen, her long chestnut hair curling over her shoulders. It was her pleasure to be helpful, obedient and obliging.

She was tall for her age. One would have taken Maria to be fourteen or fifteen. She was slender and graceful, and with the black shawl over her shoulders, she looked more like the young lady of tomorrow. But her soul was at peace, and quickly she took up each duty.

Unfortunately, Maria had never gone to school. She knew not how to read or write. Like her mother before her, she was a poor, unlettered country girl. Her prayers she learned by heart from Assunta, and now, in turn, she was teaching them to her brothers and sisters. When she made her First Communion, she was behind the others. To be the poorest, the most humble, was her lot in life. She did not realize, though, that she was likely the richest in virtue and the most loved by Him who that day had given Himself to her.

Soon that great day was slipping into memory, and it seemed as though Maria would be lost in the obscurity of the swampland, for God had chosen her to do no miraculous deeds. She heard no mysterious voices, like St. Joan of Arc, calling her to feats of battle. The bread she gave to the poor did not turn to roses in her apron, as with St. Germaine. Unlike St. Bernadette and St. Therese, Our Lady did not smile on her. Maria expected nothing. Between her morning prayer and her nightly remembrance of her father, she did only the holy will of God.

One morning, not long after her First Communion, Maria had gone down to the public well in Ferriere to draw water. While waiting for her bucket to fill, she had overheard one of the village girls telling a boy an off-color joke. Maria recognized this girl as one of her companions in the First Communion class . . . and was shocked. "How could she so soon forget Jesus?"

Hurrying home, Maria could not contain herself. Hardly was she in the door when the words tumbled out in a torrent: "Mama! Do you know . . . at the well . . . the girl said terrible things . . . and the boy laughed . . ."

"Why then did you listen?" chided her mother.

"I couldn't help it! I had to wait for the bucket to fill."

"Yes," Assunta nodded wisely. "I know you are astonished that girls and boys talk about such things. Just remember, if you were to say such things, people would be even more astonished at you."

Maria could hardly believe her ears. Did her mother really think that she would ever offend God in that dreadful way? "Talk about such things," she said with amazement in her voice. "Why, I would rather die . . ."

But all was not serious. At rare intervals there were innocent distractions in her life. On those days, with her godmother and neighbor, Theresa Cimarelli, she went to market at Nettuno to sell vegetables and eggs. Maria enjoyed those seven miles of pleasant talk, while their cart jogged along and the pigeons cooed in their cages. She who was so silent now had much to say. Maria at these times refound her childhood gaiety.

On these trips, the two would visit the Shrine of Our Lady of Grace at Nettuno, and Maria was able to pray to the Blessed Virgin before her famous image. There in a special way she could ask Mary Immaculate for grace to persevere each day in goodness, in purity . . .

Unfortunately, these hours were few and passed all too quickly. Tomorrow she would take up her daily routine again. Tomorrow she would muster her courage and begin anew, without complaint, the same old tasks.

Little did this girl realize the way that God was leading her . . . and that on one of those tomorrows she would need the strength of a martyr!

—7—

THE ANGEL OF DARKNESS

It was getting close to the end of June. The day had been very sultry, and now with the night there was a bit of cool air creeping up from the swamps. Toads and frogs could be heard croaking for rain, while a hoot-owl, nestled in the hollow of an old elm, was sending forth his stupid wail into the night.

At Ferriere, behind closed doors, the kitchen fire smoldered to ashes. All was wrapped in sleep, save the white form at the bedside.

Maria had not gone to rest. Kneeling in her night-gown for evening prayer, she seemed to continue indefinitely. At the examination of conscience, she had faltered and knew not how to continue. Strange things that day had upset her soul. Examination of conscience, ordinarily so easy and rapid, had now become painful and complicated. There were things that she did not well understand. An evil she could only guess at and yet not know, troubled her. She was filled with shame and deep trouble and wondered if she had offended her God. Thoughts of Alessandro, too, frightened her.

And now, before God, she recalls everything that had happened. One day last week her mother had been too tired to work and had remained at home. She had sent Maria to take her place in the fields. It was a pleasure for the girl to help, and she had set out with Alessandro to hoe at the other end of the property. They were alone in the field now, working side by side for more than an hour. Suddenly Alessandro, throwing aside his hoe, crossed the furrow that separated them and stood before her.

He seemed beside himself. His eyes were alight with a strange fire. He seized Maria by the arms, stammering words that she could not grasp. She was stupefied, unable to understand what he wanted. Then it suddenly dawned on her that he was soliciting her to sin. Indignation brought the blood to her face. Violently she shook herself free and fled down the field. She hid herself in a hedge till noon, and then went in for lunch. In the afternoon she pretended to return to work with him, but under the pretext of getting a basket in the barn, had climbed to the loft and buried herself in the hay, where she remained motionless for three hours.

For a whole week she had thus avoided him. Never would she let herself be caught alone with him. She seemed confident he would not try again.

But this morning he had surprised her. She had been making the beds. There was no one in the house. He had entered from behind and taken hold of her. She had sunk her nails into his face until he cursed in pain and let her go. Immediately she had started for the door to call for help, but he was there before her and silenced her with a threat:

"If you say a word to your mother, I'll kill you."
And he shook his fist before her frightened eyes.

Alessandro had gone out, and she had locked herself in her room. She feared he might return and so she was afraid even to go to the kitchen to prepare the meal. When, through the window, she saw her mother returning from work, she hurried to start the fire. But it was too late. The soup was not warm by noon and she had not had time to set the table. She received a harsh scolding. Alessandro, seated before an empty plate, laughed and made sport of her.

How it pained her! Once she thought she would tell all. The words were there on her tongue, but she bit her lip. What was the use? Her poor mother could do nothing. And if the evil intentions of Alessandro were known, there would be more wranglings with the Serenellis. Life would become unbearable. Then, too, he had said he would kill her. It would be best to keep her secret to herself.

But tonight at her bedside, reliving the painful hours of this sad day, she was unable to keep back her tears. Her whole body trembled, and a wave of fear swept over her. Her throat was dry and tense. She buried her head in the covers, and her prayer terminated in bitter sobs.

This was not a childish vexation. From now on, the soul of Maria is different. A veil of sadness clouds her eyes. Her smile is gone. There is nothing left of the little girl, neither laughter nor the playfulness that at times betrayed her eleven years.

She understands at last. Her actions are measured, her words are rare. She avoids sitting down at the common table and flees Alessandro as one might flee a plague.

But he seeks her out, as she well perceives. He waits, he watches, he follows her about the house. The cat and mouse story has begun. It is a duel unsuspected even by Assunta. Maria becomes increasingly reticent. The terrible threat rings in her ears, and each time she sees Alessandro, she reads in his eyes: "If you speak, I'll kill you."

From now on Maria lives under a reign of terror. Formerly, when she was small, the ghost stories of her father did not even frighten her; she laughed heartily at them. When she was eight, she was not afraid to cross the yard in blackest night to shut the door of the hen house. And on the way to Mass at Conca, she would run ahead of the rest to beat off the snakes that lay in their path. She could not remember ever having been afraid. But now, whenever she is alone, an indefinable anguish chills her heart. Alessandro might come back. Alessandro might surprise her. Alessandro might overcome her. She feels so weak.

But no. A voice in prayer reassures her and tells her she is strong.

Who shall be able to overcome God living in her heart?

—8—

EVEN TO BLOOD

It is once more high noon. The sun from its zenith beats down on the Ferriere farm. A burning wind, storm-laden, sweeps across the swamps, licks the walls of the house and enters the kitchen by the open door.

The Gorettis and Serenellis as usual are seated about the table. They have just finished their lunch. It is so hot that they delay a bit before returning to work. If Giovanni would permit, they would gladly take their siesta. But he insists on working immediately after lunch, and they await his orders. Maria is doing dishes, amidst a silence broken only by the clatter of the plates.

Hay and straw are already in the barn, but the unthrashed beans are still spread out in the yard, drying in the sun.

"Go harness the team!" Giovanni orders. "There is no time to lose! We will have rain this afternoon. The beans will have to be in beforehand."

Slowly Alessandro and Angelo rise. Assunta clears the table and pushes the benches beneath it. The other children scamper out of doors. Giovanni alone does not move. "Put the beans in bags and take them up to the loft!" he continues.

But Alessandro does not hear his father. He has another project in mind. For the past hour his eyes have followed Maria. Before returning to work, he goes to his room, where he is heard fumbling in his closet.

"Maria, I have a torn shirt that needs mending," he calls out. "I'll need it to go to Mass tomorrow. You'll have to repair it for me this afternoon. I'm leaving it here for you." And this he says with studied nonchalance.

The dishwashing stopped, but there was no reply. Within the girl's heart emotions struggled for expression. She felt like crying: "No! I have no time . . ." and it would have relieved her. But in spite of an instinctive repugnance, she consented again to be of service. True charity won out in her heart.

While he was harnessing the oxen in the stable, Alessandro's thoughts pursued their evil trend. His plans took definite shape. He visualized the scene. Maria will be quietly seated, and there will be nobody in the house but the baby, Theresa. He will hurry in, close the kitchen door, then lock the door. It will be so easy.

"Giddap!" he calls to the oxen. Then leaping on the cart, he drives out into the yard.

For want of a thrasher, the Gorettis had improvised a method of their own. The beanstalks were heaped in the yard, and the cart, loaded with youngsters, passed and repassed over the piles. Meanwhile, Assunta turned and shook the lot with her fork.

Poor mother, her heart was full as she paused from time to time to witness the joy of her little ones. "Look at Angelo," she mused, "so like his father directing the cart. What a consolation he is to me—my eldest. If we can only carry on for a little while longer, perhaps things will be brighter. Then, too, there's my Maria, so good to everyone! She is so sweet and holy. Maybe she's a little too reserved. For the past month—especially since her First Communion—she seems to be timid and worried. She hardly speaks, and her eyes are always downcast. She blushes so easily— her prayers are prolonged. What can be taking place in her soul? Apparently she has some secret . . . but then, she is at that age when girls are easily disturbed."

Thus, while the oxen turn on the thrashing floor and the children shout and laugh, Assunta pursues the thread of her maternal love—her only joy on earth. Suddenly Alessandro stops the cart and jumps down. "Take my place for awhile," he tells Assunta, "I forgot my handkerchief in my room. I'll be right back." His forehead is moist with sweat.

Obediently Assunta puts aside her fork and climbs up in his place. The cart is off again, and the joy of children and mother is doubled.

Then as Alessandro disappears through the door-way, a flash of lightning is seen on the horizon and a clap of thunder follows. The storm is approaching. The noon-day devil prowls about the Ferriere farm.

Meanwhile, Maria is seated on the porch above

the kitchen door. It is much too hot within the house. She has taken Alessandro's shirt and found a whole sleeve torn. It will be a long job, but courageously she sets about it and her needle flies to and fro. Beside her on a blanket her baby sister, Theresa, is fast asleep. From the other side of the house the racket and noise of the thrashing assure her of contentment and hope. Alone, she dreams of the morrow.

"Tomorrow will be Sunday, Feast of the Precious Blood. I will start early with Theresa Cimarelli," she tells herself, "so we can get to Confession and Communion."

Her little soul expands already in anticipation. She has so much to tell, so much advice to seek, such great strength to receive.

Suddenly, Alessandro looks out of the kitchen door. She jumps with apprehension. He has seen her on the porch. Up the stairway he comes and without a word passes into the bedroom. Why has he come? She can hear him fumbling with tools in the end room. What is he up to? Perhaps he has forgotten to take a sickle with him. Then he reappears in the doorway.

"Maria, come here!"

His voice is harsh, and she is thoroughly frightened. The sewing drops to her lap and she neither answers nor moves.

"Hear me! Come here immediately!" Alessandro is already very impatient. He grabs her by the arm, and though she clings to the banister and calls for help, it is of no avail. He drags her into the house and bolts the door. She is his prisoner, with little chance of escape. Maria pleads desperately, "Alessandro, let me go! Let me go!"

Alessandro holds up a knife threateningly. It has been sharpened into a pointed dagger.

With waves of fear, Maria understands his evil intentions. But in spite of the frightened sobs that climb in her throat, a supernatural energy animates her. She will resist sin to the end—even to death if need be.

Frantically Maria wrenches free and screams for help . . . but who can hear amid the noise of the cart and children and beans. She leaps around the table for protection, but he knocks it aside and trips her. As she falls, he pins her, yet she continues to struggle wildly for release. He has not expected such resistance. Maria cries out:

"No! I will not, Alessandro, no!" Her constancy seems only to enrage him. He draws the cruel knife menacingly over her.

Maria knows the danger. This brute is now capable of anything. He is getting beside himself with rage. She pleads desperately: "Alessandro, let me go! Let me go!"

The knife now hangs over her breast. She must choose: death or life, Heaven or Hell, God or Satan, sin or martyrdom. In a burst of heroism, making desperate efforts to free herself, she chooses energetically, superhumanly.

"No! No! It is a sin! God does not want this! If you do this, you will go to Hell! What are you doing, Alessandro! You will go to Hell!"

The tragedy followed. Alessandro said later that something seemed to snap within him. With mad rage, he plunged the steel into her chest and abdomen, then into her back—making fourteen wounds in all.

"It was just like I was pounding corn, like sticking a knife into a log," he said later.

Maria continued to repeat, "God does not want this! You will go to Hell!" With her right hand she tried to hold her dress modestly over her knees. Then, mercifully, she lost consciousness.

After the blows, Alessandro thought her dead. Dumbfounded, he got up. Blood had sobered him. He threw the knife behind the closet, went to his room and locked the door.

The sun was now flooding in by the window. The black clouds were scattering in the distance; the storm had passed. The cracking of bean stalks and the shouts of the children continued in the yard.

HOURS OF PAIN

Outside the thrashing carried on without respite, though less hurriedly, as the threatening storm had passed. All that remained was to separate the chaff from the grain and gather the precious harvest into the barn. In the evening, a bonfire of stalks would symbolize the family joy and abundance.

But Alessandro had not returned, baby Theresa could be heard crying on the porch, and Assunta became worried.

"Mariano, go see what is keeping Alessandro, and tell Maria to look after the baby. I'm afraid the child will fall down the stairs."

Suddenly a call resounded from the house. "Assunta! Assunta! Come here!" It was Giovanni, yelling as though the house were afire. What now? Surely something serious had happened.

The poor mother dropped everything and hurried up the stairs and into the room where Maria lay writhing in pain; close at her heels came her neighbors, Theresa Cimarelli and faithful Domenico. All were filled with confusion at the sight of Maria's bloody body and the room in disarray. Tenderly, Domenico lifted Maria and carried her into the bedroom. The sight of the limp form of her daughter was too much for poor Assunta. She grew weak and fell fainting on the floor.

When Assunta revived, Theresa was working over Maria and Giovanni was explaining his story. "I was sleeping in the shade beside the house when the baby awoke me with her crying. I didn't pay much attention to that, but then I heard Maria calling with a feeble voice from the doorway. So I got up, and just in time to see her fall in the doorway. She had fainted, so I shouted for Assunta and all of you. I don't know what happened. But look, her dress is blood-stained."

Assunta leaned over her daughter: "Maria, what has happened?"

The girl made no reply. Apparently she was suffocating. With her hands she was trying to undo her clothing. Her mother lent a hand, unhooking and loosening the blouse, and a trickle of red blood crept across her throat. With infinite precaution the two women raised her a bit and slid out her arms from the sleeves, and removed the blouse. Her underclothing was all saturated with blood.

On her breast near the heart, the thin blade had made a narrow but deep entry. Four gashes criss-crossed the stomach. The whole of that little body was horribly torn. Blood congealed about the wounds and trickled in drops upon the sheet.

The heroic child did not even whimper. It was her rest after the battle, repose after victory. Her long, disheveled hair formed an aureole beneath her head. Her discolored lips remained closed. They had not yet revealed the name of the assailant.

"Maria, my little one, tell me what has happened! Who did this to you?"

Maria hesitated a bit, then, raising her large, innocent eyes to her mother, she whispered: "It was Alessandro, Mama."

"Who? Alessandro! But why?"

Maria seemed to reflect before speaking. The whole drama repassed swiftly before her eyes. Then quietly she answered: "Because he wanted to commit an awful sin, and I would not."

There was the secret of her martyrdom. The two women dared not pry further.

Meanwhile there was much going on outside. Domenico had hitched up his cart and had hurried off to get a doctor at Nettuno. Along the way he notified neighbors, and the tragic news flew from farm to farm. "A crime committed at Ferriere; Maria attacked."

Housework, plowing, gardens and sheep were abandoned, and the whole countryside seemed to flock to "the old cheese factory." Some of the men carried pitchforks, others clubs, and still others came with rifles. No one knew what to expect.

Soon the house was thronged. Women were getting in each other's way, and everybody wanted to see the little victim. She was so sweet and good! Some wept, others whispered in little groups. With each newcomer the details were told again, and Alessandro's name was repeated over and over. The blood on the floor seemed to tell its own story.

Suddenly there was a commotion. Someone discovered the knife behind the closet. Indignation flared up, tempers grew hot. "Alessandro!" "Where is Alessandro!"

"He must be here," shouted one of the men, trying the door. "But the door is barred from the inside." Several tried to force the oak panel with their shoulders. Someone suggested getting a crowbar. Then Count Mazzoleni came rushing in. Seeing the men struggling to get at Alessandro, he tried to calm them:

"No, wait, better notify the police. They'll come and arrest him." For Mazzoleni feared that these excited men might only add murder to murder. So two of the farmers then rushed off for the police—one to Nettuno and the other to Citerna.

But so many people and such turmoil in the next room was fatiguing to Maria. In vain did she beg to be left alone with her mother and godmother. Each one thought his or her presence necessary in the room . . . Only Dr. Bartoli's arrival restored order, and everyone was put out of the house.

The doctor made his examination quickly. The case was most serious. An operation was necessary. Another messenger was sent for an ambulance to bring Maria to the hospital. First aid was administered, and with the help of bed-sheeting the poor body was bandaged temporarily.

Precious time slipped by in waiting for the ambulance, and though the others were impatient, Maria remained quiet. Her body was weakening steadily. Since two o'clock that afternoon she had been bleeding, and it was six o'clock before the horse-drawn ambulance arrived.

—10—

THE FINAL STRUGGLE

The stretcher had to be brought right up to the bedside. Maria had become limp. Painful gasps escaped her when the doctor and Domenico roused her, though they were ever so gentle. They laid her on the stretcher, covered her with a blanket, and carried her down to the ambulance at the bottom of the stairway.

Neighbors crowded around to see their Maria for the last time. Her brothers and sisters climbed into the wagon to kiss her good-bye. She was haggard, pale and disfigured. Tears welled up in her dark eyes and stole furtively down her cheeks. Assunta took her position at her head; the doctor sat up with the driver, and they were off. This was Maria's farewell to Ferriere . . . and theirs to her.

White pigeons careened overhead, turning and fluttering about the roof she called home.

Many a time Maria had traveled these seven miles of dusty road to Nettuno. Many happy trips she had made along this way with Theresa Cimarelli to sell their poultry and eggs. Other times, too, she had gone this way with her dear mother to visit the shrine of Our Lady of Grace. She had been able to laugh then and enjoy life, which seemed

pleasant in spite of hardships. But now her teeth
are clenched, her face is set and her hands clutch
the side of the stretcher. The road is rough, the
horses unsteady, and with every jolt her whole body
is dipped anew in a flood of pain.

"Are you suffering, my little one?" Assunta asks.

Maria makes an effort to smile. "Yes, Mama, a
little. Have we still far to go?"

With great effort she turns her head a little to
the side, trying to recognize some familiar land-
mark: trees along the way, the cemetery fence, the
iron cross at the fork in the road. At last they reach
the bridge over the canal—the halfway mark. How
long these seven miles seem. Pain racks her body.
Even breathing is painful. Stiffly her head returns
to the cushion; her feverish eyes stare up into the
blue heavens, which never seemed so beautiful as
now.

At a bend in the road two mounted policemen
hurried past the ambulance. Between their two
horses a handcuffed man was dragged on foot.
Assunta was not able to conceal her surprise. In
the perspiring, dust-covered runner she recognized
Alessandro. Fortunately, Maria had seen nothing.

As they entered Nettuno, crowds gathered and
escorted the ambulance. The sad story had preceded
them. The arrival of the criminal had been witnessed at the prison gates with threatening tumult.
At the Orsenigo Hospital doorway, throngs had
gathered in silent awe. Everybody wanted to see
the heroine. And they did see her, as the stretcher
was borne up the stairway. Surrounded by a wave

of chestnut hair, a beautiful, innocent face looked kindly out on them and tried to smile. When the doors of the hospital shut her from their eyes, the crowd dispersed and some were heard to murmur: "She's a real martyr." The voice of the people had already canonized Maria Goretti.

Yet she had not achieved her full measure of suffering. A second time she must experience the knife on her flesh. The hospital chaplain came to visit her on the operating table. She betrayed no concern, but gladly went to Confession. Perhaps she scarcely believed death to be near. At such an early age, one does not feel death's approach. The body is too well equipped for reaction against even the most severe suffering. As the priest was leaving, a surgeon whispered in his ear: "Where you have found an angel, I am afraid we will leave but a corpse."

Fourteen wounds were discovered, the intestines were torn, the lungs were pierced completely through and the heart grazed. The lower bone structure was seriously injured, showing four chest wounds and five in the abdominal region. Added to this were five minor gashes. Stitching and bandaging only added torture to the poor sufferer. In spite of her intense pain, she remained calm, invoking the Blessed Virgin Mary. The surgical work continued for two long hours. No anesthetic was administered because the attendants feared peritonitis. Finally, she lost consciousness.

When Assunta entered the sick-room, she thought her child was dead, and she began to cry.

Little by little, Maria recovered. Her eyelids slowly opened. She called for water, but that relief had to be denied her; she willingly accepted the sacrifice in remembrance of Jesus' thirst on the Cross. She was told not to speak, but she had difficulty in understanding that, because she felt she was much better. Her sufferings had abated somewhat. She remained motionless. Her body was completely wrapped as in a cast. Only her arms were outside the covers, but she could not move them without great pain. Her bloodless hands were cold and white and her feet like ice.

Towards ten o'clock in the evening, she seemed to be slipping into a coma. She moaned continually. Dr. Bartoli dropped in again before leaving the hospital for the night. He urged Assunta to go and take some rest. A nurse would remain with Maria. When finally the poor mother agreed to go, the noise of the chair on the stone floor awoke the sufferer. She guessed that her mother was leaving. An effort of protest came to her, but the word was not uttered. Courageous to the end, she accepted still another sacrifice.

Throughout the night, in a half-conscious state, she moaned as though hot flames bathed her body. Spasms of pain racked her nerves. Every now and then a convulsion would bring an involuntary cry to her lips. At dawn, exhausted, she fell into a labored sleep.

At five o'clock, Dr. Bartoli returned. He found her sleeping. Her respiration was regular but scarcely perceptible. A half-hour later she awoke with a groan. She seemed to remember nothing that had happened. When Assunta entered with the hospital chaplain, a light smile passed over Maria's face. She told her mother that she felt well, inquired where she had passed the night, spoke of her brothers and sisters and said she would like to see them.

Her thoughts went back to Ferriere without any fright. The name of Alessandro did not cross her lips, nor did anyone dare recall to her mind the tragic events of the preceding day.

When the priest offered to bring her Holy Communion, her face lit up with evident joy. She had been expecting that Visitor. Slowly she crossed her hands on her breast and asked her mother to raise the pillow a bit.

Her soul was ready, but there remained one more heroic act before her final tryst with God. The chaplain reminded her of how Jesus had pardoned His murderers when He died upon the Cross.

She seemed to reflect. Her eyes rested upon the crucifix on the wall. Then with voice expressive of her generous soul, she said:

"Yes, for the love of Jesus I too pardon him, and I want him to be with me in Heaven."

Assunta wept. The priest too brushed away the tears as he turned to get the Blessed Sacrament. In a few moments he was back, and Maria received her dear Jesus in Holy Viaticum.

Ten o'clock that morning Dr. Bartoli returned to change the dressings. Great violet scabs had formed about the wounds. Black and blue lumps now showed on knee, legs and elbow, indicating with

what desperate efforts the child had defended herself. But these were only slight injuries compared
to the wounds she had received. The perforation
of the intestines was especially grave. Internal hem-
orrhages were threatening blood poisoning that
could carry her off within a few hours. The doctor
saw by the failing respiration that the end was not
far off.

During the morning Sergeant Fantini came to
question the victim and draw up a charge against
Alessandro. Maria answered calmly in monosylla-
bles, without showing the least resentment. When
she was asked where the dagger had struck, she
pointed very simply to the wounds in her breast,
adding modestly, "and elsewhere." He and the cara-
biniere dared not inquire further.

When Assunta was again alone with her daughter, she asked if Alessandro had not tried to seduce
her at other times. Maria admitted simply that there
were two other attempts, which she had rejected.

"But why didn't you tell me about it?" Assunta
pleaded.

"Because he said he would kill me if I did." Then
with a sigh, "And you see, he killed me anyway."

By now Maria was failing fast. Extreme Unction
was administered, and for three hours she battled
with an invisible enemy. Her head swayed on the
pillow, her hands clenched.

"Alessandro! Alessandro, let me go . . . NO! NO!
NO! You will go to Hell! Mama, Mama, help!" The
memory of the struggle haunted her delirium.

Some moments of lucidity pierced through those

trying hours. "Mama," she said, "forgive me." The mother's answer was a mother's kiss.

The last agony began at three o'clock in the afternoon. Maria's eyes settled on the statue of Our Lady placed at the foot of her bed. Suddenly her lips stammered, "Theresa." The nurse took her icy hand: "Your baby sister is not here, Maria."

A long spasm shook her whole body, her muscles tensed, she threw back her head violently against the pillow. A long gasp seemed to tear out her lungs. Her head settled calmly on the pillow. The light in her beautiful eyes went out. Maria had breathed her last. God had already rewarded her victory.

It was July 6, 1902, the first Sunday in July, Feast of the Precious Blood. Out over the city, bells were ringing the Vesper hour. In the nearby church, Passionists were chanting the antiphon from Vespers of the Feast of the Precious Blood:

"Who is this that cometh . . . this beautiful one . . . Why then is thy apparel red, and thy garments like theirs that tread in the wine press?"

EPILOGUE

Just forty-eight years later, on June 24, 1950, a huge crowd of Holy Year pilgrims thronged the Piazza to hear His Holiness Pope Pius XII, in the first outdoor canonization ever, proclaim Maria Goretti a Saint and the new Patroness of Catholic Youth.

Looking up through tear-dimmed eyes at the magnificent picture of Maria in glory was Assunta Goretti. She was the first mother ever to witness her daughter's canonization—and did she perhaps remember in the thrill of that moment what Maria had said to cheer her in the darkest hour at Ferriere:

"Mama, why are you crying? All will be well . . . we shall be great . . . we shall have everything!"

PICTURES

The house in which St. Maria Goretti received the fatal wounds. This photo shows the staircase on which Maria was sitting when Alessandro approached.

The room of St. Maria Goretti and her sisters.

A small chapel has been built in the kitchen where St. Maria Goretti was stabbed fourteen times by Alessandro Serenelli. Alessandro later repented and asked forgiveness of God and St. Maria's mother.

This monument marks the spot where St. Maria Goretti received the fatal wounds.

This room where Maria died in the former Orseniga Hospital
has been converted into a chapel.

The facade of St. Peter's Basilica on the day of St. Maria Goretti's canonization, June 24, 1950. *Opposite:* Part of the huge crowd of Holy Year pilgrims who thronged the piazza of St. Peter's for the ceremony—the largest crowd that had ever assembled for a canonization.

57

Assunta, the first mother ever to witness her daughter's canonization, follows the ceremony from a window high in the Vatican.

St. Maria Goretti's mother views the wax figure containing her daughter's relics.

In his later years, Alessandro became very devoted to St. Maria Goretti, the young girl he had murdered, trusting in her intercession in Heaven for him. For many years Alessandro lived at a Capuchin monastery, where he worked as a gardener. He became a tertiary, or lay member of the Order. Alessandro died at the monastery in 1969, at age 87.

The wax figure which contains the relics of St. Maria Goretti.

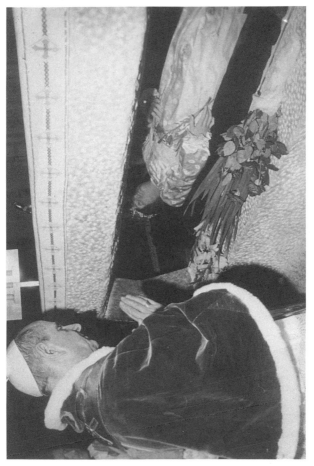

Paul VI prays before the relics of St. Maria Goretti.

Portrait of St. Maria Goretti painted by Soffredini in 1929.

Canonization banner of St. Maria Goretti in glory. (Painting by A. Bea.)

The Shrine of Our Lady of Grace and St. Maria Goretti, Nettuno.

—12—

MODEL OF YOUTH

(Homily delivered by His Holiness, Pope Pius XII, at the ceremony of Canonization of St. Maria Goretti, in the piazza of St. Peter's, June 24, 1950)

By the loving providence of God, We have assisted this evening at the supreme exaltation of a humble daughter of the people, in a ceremony whose solemnity and dignity are unique in the history of the Church. For tonight's canonization has been held in this vast and inviting place of mystery, made for the occasion into a sacred temple whose vault is the open heaven that proclaims the glories of Almighty God—a choice for which you first expressed the desire before We had decided to make the disposition.

The concourse of the faithful come here for the occasion exceeds anything that has ever been witnessed at any other canonization. You have been lured here, We might almost say, by the entrancing beauty and intoxicating fragrance of this lily mantled with crimson whom We, only a moment ago, had the intense pleasure of inscribing in the roll of the Saints: the sweet little martyr of purity, Maria Goretti.

But why, beloved children, have you come here

in such countless numbers to assist at her glorifi-
cation? Why is it that when you read or listen to
the story of her brief life, which reminds you of
the limpid narrative of the Gospels in the simplicity
of its details, in the color of its circumstances, in
the sudden violence of death with which it closes—
why does this story move you even to tears? Why
has Maria Goretti so quickly conquered your hearts,
and taken the first place in your affections?

The reason is that there is still in this world,
apparently sunk and immersed in the worship of
pleasure, not only a meager little band of chosen
souls who thirst for Heaven and its pure air, but a
crowd, nay, an immense multitude on whom the
supernatural fragrance of Christian purity exercises
an irresistible and reassuring fascination.

If it is true that in the martyrdom of Maria
Goretti there stands out above everything else her
purity, it is also true that in her and with her the
other Christian virtues are not less glorified. For
in her virtue of purity, we have the most basic and
significant confirmation of the perfect dominion of
her spirit over gross matter. In her act of supreme
heroism, which was not something unprepared, we
see an evidence of her tender and docile love, at
once obedient and practical, towards the parents
of her flesh. There was also the sacrifice she had
made in her difficult daily labor. There was the
evangelical poverty to which she freely submitted
and in which she was sustained by her confidence
in heavenly Providence. There was her religion, to
which she tenaciously clung and which she desired

to understand better with the passing of every day—which she nourished by the practice of her prayers and which thus became for her a veritable treasure in her life. There was her ardent longing to receive Jesus in the Eucharist. Finally, as the crown of her charity, there was the heroic pardon which she granted to the man who had murdered her. A rustic garland of flowers in the field—these virtues—but ever so dear to God, for they adorned the white veil of her First Communion, and shortly after, her martyrdom.

This sacred rite of canonization has really developed into a spontaneous and popular demonstration in favor of purity. For although against the light of every martyrdom there is, perforce, the ugly contrasting stain of some iniquity, behind that of Maria Goretti stands the spectacle of a scandal that at the beginning of this century was practically unnoticed.

During the past fifty years, coupled with what was often a weak reaction on the part of decent people, there has been a conspiracy of evil practices, propagating themselves in books and illustrations, in theatres and radio programs, in styles and clubs and on the beaches, trying to work their way into the heart of the family and society, and doing their worst damage among the youth, even among those of the tenderest years, in whom the possession of virtue is a natural inheritance.

Dearly beloved youth, young men and women, who are the special object of the love of Jesus and of Us, tell me, are you resolved to resist firmly, with the help of Divine grace, every attempt made to violate your chastity?

You fathers and mothers, tell me—in the presence of this vast multitude, and before the image of this young virgin, who by her inviolate candor has stolen your hearts . . . in the presence of her mother who educated her to martyrdom and who, as much as she felt the bitterness of the outrage, never complained about her daughter's death and is now moved with emotion as she invokes her— tell me, are you ready to assume the solemn duty laid upon you to watch, as far as in you lies, over your sons and daughters, to preserve and defend them against so many dangers that surround them, and to keep them always far away from places where they might learn the practices of impiety and of moral perversion?

Finally, all of you who are intently listening to Our words know that above the unhealthy marshes and filth of the world stretches an immense Heaven of beauty. It is the Heaven which fascinated little Maria, the Heaven to which she longed to ascend by the only road that leads there, which is religion, the love of Christ and the heroic observance of His Commandments.

We greet you, O beautiful and loveable Saint! Martyr on earth and Angel in Heaven, look down from your glory on this people which loves you, which venerates, glorifies and exalts you. On your forehead you bear the full brilliant and victorious name of Christ. In your virginal countenance may be read the strength of your love and the constancy of your fidelity to your Divine Spouse. As His bride espoused in blood, you have traced in yourself His own image.

To you, therefore, powerful intercessor with the Lamb of God, we entrust these Our sons and daughters who are present here, and those countless others who are united with Us in spirit. For while they admire your heroism, they are even more desirous of imitating your strength of faith and your inviolate purity of conduct. Fathers and mothers have recourse to you, asking you to help them in their task of education. In you, through Our hands, the children and all young people will find a safe refuge, trusting that they shall be protected from every contamination and be able to walk the highways of life with that serenity of spirit and deep joy which is the heritage of those who are pure of heart. Amen.

NOVENA TO
ST. MARIA GORETTI

Based upon the Canonization Homily
of Pope Pius XII

INTRODUCTION

This Novena has been written primarily to mark the first observance of the Feast of St. Maria Goretti following her Canonization during the Holy Year (June 24, 1950). On that occasion the Holy Father proposed the little Maid of Corinaldo as a model for the youth of our times. Earlier, he had termed her "the modern St. Agnes."

His Holiness Pope Pius XII is keenly aware of the temptations to which his young flock all over the world is subjected, and he knows that the vice of impurity seeks to destroy the flower of our youth.

The Novena begins June 28 and ends on July 6, Feast of St. Maria Goretti. The prayers are based

Publisher's Note (1998): This novena is from the booklet *Novena to St. Mary Goretti*, by Father Conroy, published by Our Sunday Visitor, Inc., Huntington, Indiana in 1951.

Nihil obstat: Rev. Edward A. Miller
                   Censor librorum
Imprimatur: ✠ Leo A. Pursley, D.D.
                   Bishop of Fort Wayne-South Bend

upon the Holy Father's never-to-be-forgotten Canonization sermon, and quotations from this are used throughout the Novena as a guide for each day's prayer. The prayers are intended to reflect the prayerful desires of His Holiness for the youth of our times and are written with their temptations in mind. Each day is dedicated to the attainment of a different virtue, though the overall intention of the Novena is for purity.

It is hoped that those who make this Novena will be able to attend Mass and receive Holy Communion daily. However, if this is not possible, one could still make the Novena by saying the required prayers. Coming as it does at the beginning of summer, the Novena to St. Maria Goretti should prove useful in alerting the minds of youth to the spiritual danger lurking in the vacation days ahead.

Though the booklet is designed for the dates mentioned above, nevertheless the Novena prayers could be said on any other successive nine days of the year. Here also are to be found other prayers which youth could use to good advantage.

—Father Conroy
June 24, 1951
First Anniversary of
the Canonization of
St. Maria Goretti

—FIRST DAY—

Purity

*". . . there stands out above everything
else her purity . . ."*

MOST lovable little Saint, who valued your
purity above any earthly gain and who sealed
this choice with a martyr's death, obtain for me
also a strong love of this virtue, so consoling to
the Sacred Heart of Jesus and to the Immaculate
Heart of Mary. The pleasures of the world create
many temptations for me. I turn to your powerful
intercession in Heaven, so that with this help I
may remain ever loyal to God, no matter what the
price. In danger, inspire me to repeat with you,
"No, it is a sin!" Amen.

Sweet Heart of Jesus, be my Love!

Sweet Heart of Mary, be my salvation!

(Turn to pages 81-84 for Concluding Prayers.)

Obedience

". . . We see an evidence of her tender and docile love, at once obedient and practical, towards the parents of her flesh."

DEAR St. Maria Goretti, model of loving obedience to parents, teach me to imitate your example. Help me to overcome all selfishness and stubborn pride; draw my parents to thee, then lead me to accept their authority as the Voice of God in my life. Help them to direct me aright, and enable me to obey their every wish. Amen.

Sweet Heart of Jesus, be my Love!

Sweet Heart of Mary, be my salvation!

(Turn to pages 81-84 for Concluding Prayers.)

Self-Denial

"There was also the sacrifice she had made in her difficult daily labor."

DEAR little St. Maria! You were ready for the moment of martyrdom because your short life was given over to daily and heroic self-denial. Your great love of the Sacred Hearts made all this possible. Teach me to love Jesus and His Blessed Mother, so that I too will be inspired to daily self-denial. I am inclined to pamper myself, to gratify my senses and to excuse myself from penance. This keeps me from being a true follower of Christ. Help me, lovable little Martyr, to a sincere practice of self-denial, so that I may be your worthy follower and thus gain Heaven for all Eternity. Amen.

Sweet Heart of Jesus, be my Love!

Sweet Heart of Mary, be my salvation!

(Turn to pages 81-84 for Concluding Prayers.)

—FOURTH DAY—

—FOURTH DAY—

Contented Living

"There was the evangelical poverty to which she freely submitted . . ."

DEAR little Saint! Your days were spent in the filth of the marshes, willingly helping your desperately poor parents and family. Obtain for me the grace to accept my present circumstances in life, no matter how difficult or humiliating they may be. "Just one little drop of water" was the only request that fell from your parched lips during those last horrible hours of life. How much I demand, and how unhappy I am when I cannot have my share of the world's conveniences and gaudy attractions! Teach me by your heroic example to be content with what I have, and to be grateful for the blessings which God has already showered upon me. Amen.

Sweet Heart of Jesus, be my Love!

Sweet Heart of Mary, be my salvation!

(Turn to pages 81-84 for Concluding Prayers.)

Confidence in God

". . . she was sustained by her confidence in heavenly Providence . . ."

DEAR little Saint, I depend a great deal upon the help of my friends in time of trouble or sorrow. I look for their approval in many things that I do. I am disconsolate and lonely when they desert me. Through your powerful intercession in Heaven, obtain for me the grace to place all my confidence in God. Only by walking constantly in His presence and depending upon His help will I have the courage to stand up for His laws, even though it may mean loss of friends, criticism and complete removal of worldly comfort. Help me to look for all my strength in Him. Amen.

Sweet Heart of Jesus, be my Love!

Sweet Heart of Mary, be my salvation!

(Turn to pages 81-84 for Concluding Prayers.)

Respect for Teachers

"There was her religion, to which she tenaciously clung and which she desired to understand better with the passing of every day . . ."

DEAR little Saint! Help me to greater love of my Faith. I have many God-given opportunities to study it, but, sad to say, I neglect them. I am even critical of the priests, brothers and sisters who offer their lives that I may better know and love my holy religion. Dear St. Maria Goretti, teach me to be thankful for these graces, which you did not have. Make me proud of my Faith and ready to die for it, if God should require that of me. Amen.

Sweet Heart of Jesus, be my Love!

Sweet Heart of Mary, be my salvation!

(Turn to pages 81-84 for Concluding Prayers.)

—SEVENTH DAY—

Love of Holy Communion

*"There was her ardent longing to receive
Jesus in the Eucharist."*

DEAR little Saint, never was Jesus more welcome in a human heart than in yours. The
Great Day of First Communion could not come
quickly enough. In borrowed clothes, and with head
crowned with flowers of the field, you knelt to
receive Him into your soul, so rich with innocence
and love, and this after months of keen anticipation!

O powerful intercessor with the Lamb of God,
inflame my soul with your "ardent longing to
receive Jesus in the Eucharist." Obtain for me the
grace to put aside laziness and indifference, so that
I may often, even daily, allow myself to be con-
sumed in the "burning Furnace of Charity." Teach
me what true Love really is! Amen.

Sweet Heart of Jesus, be my Love!

Sweet Heart of Mary, be my salvation!

(Turn to pages 81-84 for Concluding Prayers.)

Charity to Others

". . . as the crown of her charity, there was the heroic pardon which she granted to the man who had murdered her."

DEAR little Martyr! To the last you followed your beloved Jesus! While hanging upon His Cross of suffering, He uttered through parched lips, "Father, forgive them, for they know not what they do!" And you upon your bed of pain, burning with fever, forgave your murderer with the words, "I too pardon him . . . I too wish him to join me in Paradise!"

Grant me the grace, O heroic Saint, to be charitable to others! Much of my time is spent on vengeful thoughts, seeking how I may pay back others the harm they have done to me. Teach me to forgive, so that I may not only gain Heaven, but also lead others there, who might otherwise be doomed to Hell. As I am to follow Christ, help me to imitate His charity, even as you have done. Amen.

Sweet Heart of Jesus, be my Love!

Sweet Heart of Mary, be my salvation!

(Turn to pages 81-84 for Concluding Prayers.)

Love of Our Blessed Mother

*"In you . . . all young people will find
a safe refuge . . ."*

DEAR St. Maria Goretti! Once again I turn
to you, and I beg of you, in the words of our
Holy Father, that "serenity of spirit and deep joy
which is the heritage of those who are pure of
heart."

Help me to turn to our Blessed Lady, confident
in the hope that she will take my hand as she did
yours and lead me on to Paradise, my heavenly
country, there to enjoy with you and her the com-
pany of God the Father, Son and Holy Ghost for
all Eternity. Amen.

Sweet Heart of Jesus, be my Love!

Sweet Heart of Mary, be my salvation!

(Turn to pages 81-84 for Concluding Prayers.)

The Litany of the Blessed Virgin Mary
(The Litany of Loreto)
(For public or private use.)

Lord, have mercy on us.
  Christ, have mercy on us.
Lord, have mercy on us. Christ, hear us.
  Christ, graciously hear us.
God the Father of Heaven,
  Have mercy on us.
God the Son, Redeemer of the world,
  Have mercy on us.
God the Holy Ghost,
  Have mercy on us.
Holy Trinity, One God,
  Have mercy on us.

Holy Mary, *pray for us.*
Holy Mother of God, *pray for us.*
Holy Virgin of virgins, *etc.*
Mother of Christ,
Mother of divine grace,
Mother most pure,
Mother most chaste,
Mother inviolate,

Mother undefiled,
Mother most amiable,
Mother most admirable,
Mother of good counsel,
Mother of our Creator,
Mother of our Saviour,
Virgin most prudent,
Virgin most venerable,
Virgin most renowned,
Virgin most powerful,
Virgin most merciful,
Virgin most faithful,
Mirror of justice,
Seat of wisdom,
Cause of our joy,
Spiritual vessel,
Vessel of honor,
Singular vessel of devotion,
Mystical rose,
Tower of David,
Tower of ivory,
House of gold,
Ark of the Covenant,
Gate of Heaven,
Morning star,
Health of the sick,
Refuge of sinners,
Comforter of the afflicted,
Help of Christians,
Queen of Angels,
Queen of patriarchs,
Queen of prophets,

Queen of Apostles,
Queen of martyrs,
Queen of confessors,
Queen of virgins,
Queen of all Saints,
Queen conceived without Original Sin,
Queen assumed into Heaven,
Queen of the most holy Rosary,
Queen of peace,

Lamb of God, Who takes away the sins of the world,
    Spare us, O Lord.
Lamb of God, Who takes away the sins of the world,
    Graciously hear us, O Lord.
Lamb of God, Who takes away the sins of the world,
    Have mercy on us.

V. Pray for us, O holy Mother of God,
R. *That we may be made worthy of the promises of Christ.*

Let Us Pray

Grant, we beseech Thee, O Lord God, that we Thy servants may enjoy perpetual health of mind and body, and by the glorious intercession of the Blessed Mary, ever Virgin, be delivered from present sorrow and enjoy everlasting happiness. Through Christ Our Lord. R. *Amen.*

Official Prayer to
St. Maria Goretti

O ST. Maria Goretti, who, strengthened by God's grace, did not hesitate, even at the age of twelve, to shed your blood and to sacrifice life itself to defend your virginal purity, look graciously on the unhappy human race, which has strayed far from the path of eternal salvation. Teach us all, and especially youth, with what courage and promptitude we should flee, for the love of Jesus, anything that could offend Him or stain our souls with sin. Obtain for us from Our Lord victory in temptation, comfort in the sorrows of life, and the grace which we earnestly beg of thee (*here insert your intention*); and may we one day enjoy with thee the imperishable glory of Heaven. Amen.

Our Father . . . Hail Mary . . . Glory be . . .

St. Maria Goretti, pray for us!

(*End of Novena prayers*)

—ADDITIONAL PRAYERS—

Prayer during Vacation

DEAR St. Maria Goretti! With added time on my hands, the danger to my soul is now greater than ever. My thoughts tend to wander and to dwell on suggestions put there by Satan himself. My imagination is stirred by the loose living I see all around me. My body resents being aroused to useful activity and craves far too much ease. Teach me, O little Saint, how to make every minute count for Eternity.

O little Saint, whose twelve short years were so fruitful for Eternity, teach me the value of keeping my mind and body usefully occupied, so that by imitating your example, I too may reach my Heavenly Home. Amen.

Our Father . . . Hail Mary . . . Glory be . . .

St. Maria Goretti, pray for us!

Prayer before a Dance or Party

DEAR St. Maria Goretti! The world teaches that we must please others in order to be popular. Our Lord requires that I please Him rather than one who asks an evil thing in the name of false love. Grant that I may have the courage to resist any temptation to sinful conduct. Teach me by your example to instill into others a real respect for modesty and purity. Through your powerful intercession, help me to make of this evening an occasion for helping others to become spiritually stronger. Grant that others may see in me reason to change their ways, if that be necessary. Let others be led closer to Jesus and Mary by my example.

O little Saint, who wanted to be popular only with your Divine Master and His Blessed Mother, help me to imitate you. Amen.

Our Father . . . Hail Mary . . . Glory be . . .

St. Maria Goretti, pray for us!

Prayer for Help against Temptations

DEAR little St. Maria Goretti! Teach me that God must be my first love, and that all other love is based on Him and Him alone. Obtain for me the grace not to toy with the occasions of sin, and to remember that my body and the bodies of all in grace are temples of the Holy Ghost, destined someday for a glorious resurrection.

Through your beautiful example, teach me the value and dignity of Christian modesty. Grant that I may never be the occasion of dragging others into Hell by suggestive words or evil deeds of any kind. Through the merits of your martyrdom, obtain for me the grace to turn aside from sin, no matter what the cost, so that one day I may enjoy Heaven with you and all the other Saints. Amen.

Our Father . . . Hail Mary . . . Glory be . . .

St. Maria Goretti, pray for us!

If you have enjoyed this book, consider making your next selection from among the following . . .

Prices subject to change.

Prices subject to change.

At your Bookdealer or direct from the Publisher.
Toll-Free 1-800-437-5876   **Fax 815-226-7770**
Tel. 815-226-7777   **www.tanbooks.com**
Prices subject to change.

ABOUT THE AUTHOR

 Born in 1920, Fr. Godfrey Poage, C.P. began writing back in college when he was looking for an easy way to make a dollar. Writing seemed the answer, so under a pseudonym he tackled the lovelorn column in his hometown paper, the Des Moines *Register & Tribune*. The success he achieved in this field encouraged him in later years to develop religious topics.

In 1939 he entered the Passionist Congregation, being ordained in 1946. His work over the ensuing years has mainly involved youth, particularly vocations, although he has also worked with the Cana program in Chicago, given parish missions and retreats, worked for the Passionist development office and served as a hospital chaplain.

Fr. Poage was called to Rome in 1956, and from 1957-1970 he worked personally with Pius XII, John XXIII and Paul VI in the Pontifical Office for Priestly and Religious Vocations. Under John XXIII and Paul VI he was in effect Director of Vocations for the entire Church.

Fr. Poage has written numerous works on vocations, Catholic Action and marriage counselling. His book on St. Maria Goretti is probably his most famous work. He appears in the video documentary on the Saint entitled *Fourteen Flowers of Pardon*. In 1962 Fr. Poage was honored with the title of Monsignor. At present he resides with the Passionist Congregation in Pasadena and is engaged in writing his memoirs.